SEALs
The Navy's Elite Force

capstone
classroom

BTR Zone (Bridge to Reading) is published by Capstone Classroom, 1710 Roe Crest Drive, North Mankato, Minnesota 56003
www.capstoneclassroom.com

ISBN: 978-1-62521-010-4

Editorial Credits
Luke Colins, editor; Kazuko Collins, layout artist; Eric Gohl, media researcher

Photo Credits
AP Photo: Sayyid Azim, 28; Corbis: 7, epa/T. Mughal, 34, Ralf-Finn Hestoft, 16, San Francisco Chronicle/Lance Iversen, 14; Courtesy of the White House: 38; Getty Images: Authenticated News/U.S. Navy, 9, Scott Olson, 19; Library of Congress: 31; Newscom: Getty Images/AFP/Ursula Coyote, 36, UPI/MC2 Michelle Kapica, 20; Public Domain: cover, 4 (all), 10, 13, 22, 24, 26, 27, 32–33, 41, 42, 43

Design Elements: Shutterstock

About the Cover
Navy SEALs practice a beach landing for a mission.

Printed in the United States of America in North Mankato, Minnesota.
012013   007111BTR

TABLE OF
CONTENTS

CHAPTER 1

SEALs in Action

Dawn is still a few hours away. Your teammates are beside you on the small seacraft. Hearts are racing. But there is no fear.

You are starting your mission aboard a STAB (SEAL Team Assault Boat). This will take you to the drop site. You know what the weather will be. You know what the beach and water conditions will be like. Your team is equipped with long-range **sniper** rifles and AK-47s. You also have equipment to communicate. Perhaps most important, you have your buddies' backs. You know they have yours.

You have spent months training for this. You'll have to get past the enemy's defenses. Your mission is to capture the target and return to the drop site. You and your team must do all of this without raising alarm.

You and your team are the best. You are young and in great shape physically and mentally. You are ready. Good luck, men. Hooyah!

sniper · a soldier trained to shoot at long-distance targets from a hidden place

The Navy SEALs trace their beginnings back to World War II (1939–1945). During this war there was a need for warriors who had the best skills or **techniques**. Some were expert shooters with a variety of guns and other **weaponry**. Some could plant underwater explosives. Some were expert raiders. They were all experts in various parts of warfare. All could get in and out of tight spots quickly and safely.

But they were not yet called SEALs. They had different names. Among the groups were the Scouts and Raiders and the Naval Combat Demolition Units. There were also the Underwater Demolition Teams (UDTs) and the Motor Torpedo Boat Squadrons.

None of those special naval groups from World War II are around today. But their bravery and skills are seen in today's SEALs.

technique · a method or way of doing something that requires skill

weaponry · a collection of weapons

an Underwater Demolition Team in 1947

UDTs were also used during the Korean War (1950–1953). They often went ahead of landing craft before a battle began. They looked for areas where boats might land. They watched for areas where boats might get stuck in mud. They searched for mines and marked them so they could be destroyed. The UDTs also planted underwater explosives and did river **surveillance**, watching for any sign of the enemy. Their missions were on land and sea.

In 1962 U.S. President John F. Kennedy created special military forces. These were fighters trained in unusual warfare **tactics**. They were prepared to fight any type of battle. The SEALs were officially given their name—the U.S. Navy Sea, Air, and Land Teams (SEALs).

surveillance · the act of keeping very close watch on someone, someplace, or something

tactic · a plan for fighting a battle

SEALs land in Vietnam in 1967.

SEAL Team 1 and SEAL Team 2 were formed from volunteers from the UDTs. Lieutenant Roy Boehm was the officer-in-charge of SEAL Team 2. It was his job to select the first group of men. He set up their training and equipment. He was given the assignment to make the first SEAL Team. Lieutenant Boehm is known as "First SEAL."

CHAPTER 2

What Does It Take to Be a SEAL?

SEALs are a special breed of men. To be a SEAL, you must be a man of strong character and high honor. You must never be unsure or **waver** in your beliefs and actions. People know they can trust you. You must be a leader. You must be able to take orders.

A SEAL is very smart. He thinks quickly. He is willing to try new plans of attack. A SEAL must be willing to take responsibility for his actions. He cannot blame others for his mistakes. Failure is not accepted by a SEAL.

A SEAL feels it is a great honor to serve his country. He wants to be the best.

Women in the Navy

Women are not allowed to serve as Navy SEALs. However, they can serve in the U.S. Navy. Alene Duerk was named the Navy's first female rear admiral in 1972. She was a nurse during World War II, the Korean War, and the Vietnam War (1959–1975). She served her country with great honor. She saved many lives.

waver · to be unsteady

What Does a SEAL Do?

SEALs perform special missions. These might be raids, surprise **ambushes**, or assaults. They might have to go under cover of darkness to capture or kill an enemy.

SEALs may be called on to collect secret information. They have to observe and report on enemy activity. This is called **reconnaissance**. SEALs also take action against terrorist groups. Sometimes SEALs must use their swimming skills. They may have to plant explosives underwater. They may need to make an **amphibious** landing where they are dropped off in the water and swim to land. All this can be very dangerous. But SEALs are not afraid. They are well trained.

Sometimes SEALs work with other countries. The SEALs help the countries train and prepare soldiers to defend their nations.

ambush · a surprise attack

reconnaissance · a mission to gather information about an enemy

amphibious · operating on both land and water

SEALs practice a secret beach landing.

It is not easy to become a SEAL. SEALs must be men who are 28 years old or younger. They must have good vision. They also have to be United States **citizens**.

Every man who wants to be a SEAL must pass an ASVAB. This is a test that measures different skills that they have. It also determines how well a person will do in the military.

Men who want to be SEALs must also pass a physical test. It includes push-ups, sit-ups, and pull-ups. They also have to swim 500 yards (457 meters) and run fast.

SEAL training takes 30 months. That is two and a half years. But if they finish, the men will be among the few who can call themselves SEALs. Today there are only 2,290 **active-duty** SEALs.

citizen · a member of a country or state who has the right to live there

active-duty · working in the military now

Recruits improve their physical fitness on an indoor obstacle course.

CHAPTER 3

SEAL Training

SEAL **recruits** begin their training at Naval Special Warfare **Preparatory** School in Great Lakes, Illinois. This training can take up to four weeks. Here recruits prepare for **boot camp**. There is tough training ahead. They build friendships and confidence. These will help the recruits as they train.

recruit · a new member of a group

preparatory · to get ready

boot camp · a place for training new members

Recruits begin physical training on an obstacle course and in the water. They train in a gym with weights. They practice how to avoid injuries.

The prep school ends when a recruit can swim 1,000 yards (914 m) with **fins** in 20 minutes. He must do 70 push-ups in two minutes. He has to do 60 sit-ups in two minutes. A recruit must do 10 pull-ups without touching the floor. Finally, he must run 4 miles (6 kilometers) wearing boots and pants in 31 minutes.

Recruits head next to BUD/S. BUD/S stands for Basic Underwater **Demolition**/SEAL. This training is in Coronado, California. BUD/S training will test recruits physically and mentally.

fin · a long, flat attachment worn on the foot to help a person swim

demolition · blowing up or taking down a structure on purpose

Recruits spend a lot of time swimming. As SEALs they will need to be confident in the water.

First Phase: Conditioning

First Phase lasts seven weeks. Recruits continue to improve physically and mentally. They can do more sit-ups, push-ups, and pull-ups than before. They develop better water skills. Their minds become sharper. They begin to see that by building a team they are able to finish their goals.

Recruits battle waves and lack of sleep during Hell Week.

The fourth week of this phase is called Hell Week. It is a five-and-a-half-day test. Each recruit must run more than 200 miles (322 km) during this test. He must also do more than 20 hours of physical activity. He will be given only four hours of sleep during the entire test. More than five days of testing with only four hours of sleep.

When a recruit has finished, he understands better what it takes to be a SEAL. He understands what commitment means. He knows about dedication. He understands what teamwork is all about.

Why Do It?

"Am I crazy?" "Why am I doing this?" These are just a few of the questions recruits think as they go through Hell Week.

Why would anyone go through so much pain and torture? Pushing your body to its limits. Pushing your mind further than it has ever gone before. At the end, you know that you did something special.

Second Phase: Combat Diving

Second Phase lasts seven weeks. Recruits begin their underwater training. They become good **scuba divers**. By the end of this phase recruits will be very comfortable in the water. They will know how to handle difficult conditions.

During Third Phase recruits practice missions and learn how to fight on land.

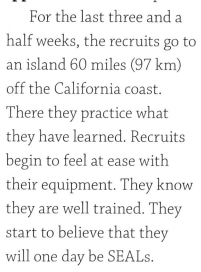

Third Phase: Land Warfare Training

This phase takes seven weeks to complete. The recruits learn about the basic weapons they will use. They will study demolition systems to understand how to take down buildings or bridges. They will begin to learn about map reading. They will learn how to **patrol** or walk an area to keep it safe. They will also learn how to **rappel** or slide down ropes.

For the last three and a half weeks, the recruits go to an island 60 miles (97 km) off the California coast. There they practice what they have learned. Recruits begin to feel at ease with their equipment. They know they are well trained. They start to believe that they will one day be SEALs.

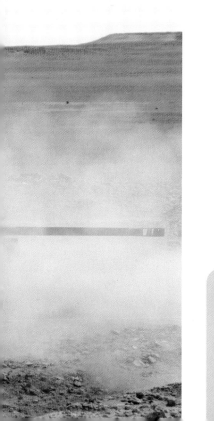

scuba diver · a person who swims underwater with air tanks for breathing

patrol · to walk or travel through an area to protect it or to keep watch

rappel · to slide down a strong rope

23

Recruits learn how to survive in cold-weather conditions.

SEAL Qualification Training (SQT)

The recruits are now on to the next phase of training. SEAL **Qualification** Training (SQT) will continue to expand their skills and knowledge.

Recruits will learn about advanced weapons. They continue training in demolitions and finding their way in new areas. They will do cold-weather training in Kodiak, Alaska.

Recruits also learn medical skills. They must be able to treat themselves if they get hurt during a mission. They must also be prepared to give medical aid to others. Their lives and the lives of their buddies may depend on it.

qualification · a skill or ability that makes a person prepared to do a job or task

A recruit practices a free-fall parachute jump.

Recruits now begin their jump-school training. They learn how to do different types of parachute jumps. They also learn how to avoid enemies and escape from them.

Upon finishing this phase of training, the recruits become true SEALs. They take part in a special ceremony. They receive the SEAL Trident. This pin shows that the man is a true Navy SEAL. He is assigned to a SEAL team. Now the team waits and trains for its first mission. They are elite warriors! Hooyah!

SEALs must be expert fighters in the sea, in the air, and on land.

A bomb set by al-Qaida ripped through the capital and U.S. embassy in the country of Kenya in 1998.

CHAPTER 4

War on Terrorism

Al-Qaida is a Muslim group that uses violence to spread its message. Muslims follow the religion of Islam. Al-Qaida was formed around 1988. It wants to get rid of U.S. power in Islamic countries.

Many al-Qaida attacks have been against places where Americans live or work. On August 7, 1998, al-Qaida bombed two U.S. **embassies** or buildings where U.S. leaders worked in Africa. The bombings killed 258 people. Among those killed were two former Navy SEALs. More than 5,000 people were hurt.

On October 12, 2000, a U.S. ship was in a harbor in Aden, Yemen. The ship was getting more fuel. Al-Qaida terrorists came beside the ship in a small boat. They set off explosives. Seventeen sailors were killed or injured.

People around the world were angry about the attack. Americans were especially angry. They made a promise to catch the people responsible. They had to be brought to justice. Their leader, Osama bin Laden, had to be found.

embassy · a building where representatives from another country work

29

September 11

On September 11, 2001, two planes flew into the two towers of the World Trade Center in New York City. Another plane flew into the Pentagon building near Washington, D.C. A fourth plane was stopped from crashing into another building. It crashed in a field in the state of Pennsylvania. These planes had been **hijacked** or taken over by force. These events became known as 9-11.

Thousands of people were killed. Thousands of people were hurt. The entire world was in shock. How could this happen?

Al-Qaida was guilty. The group claimed responsibility for the attacks. Its **terrorists,** or members who frighten people to spread a message, trained openly in the United States. They lived freely in the United States for many months while they prepared for their attacks. But the United States began to fight back.

The United States has always had a federal Department of Homeland Security. This agency handled natural disasters. But after 9-11 its work was expanded. Now it hunts terrorists inside the United States. It also makes sure its borders are secure.

hijack · to take control of a vehicle by force

terrorist · someone who uses violence and threats to frighten people into obeying

Almost 3,000 people were killed in the 9-11 terrorist attacks.

The Hunt for Osama bin Laden

Osama bin Laden was the leader of al-Qaida. He was the number 1 terrorist target for the United States. He had to be stopped. This was just the type of mission that the SEALs were trained to handle.

Several U.S. government organizations gathered information about Osama bin Laden. The SEALs used their own skills to collect information. This type of information is hard to get. But that did not stop the SEALs. They continued to search caves and desert hiding places in the countries of Afghanistan and Pakistan. They searched where their information took them.

The SEALs searched, but each time Osama bin Laden got away. But that did not stop the SEALs from searching. Bin Laden was hiding and on the run. The SEALs were closing in.

CHAPTER 5

Target: Osama bin Laden

In July 2010 the SEALs learned that Osama bin Laden was probably in Abbottabad, Pakistan. He was hiding in a large house there.

The SEALs had to know for sure. They had to find out bin Laden's habits. When did he come to the house? When did he leave? Who was with him? What kind of weapons did they have?

All these questions and more had to be studied. The SEALs had to have a plan. They do not do an operation like this without a lot of research, study, and training.

The Navy built the SEALs a full-scale model of the house they thought bin Laden was using. This allowed the SEALs to practice their mission. How would they get in? How would they get out? Who would they have to fight?

The house Osama bin Laden hid in was surrounded by high walls.

SEAL Team 6 attacked at night, surprising the people inside.

SEAL Team 6 was finally ready to go. They were well prepared. Details for the mission had been arranged. On April 29, 2012, at 8:30 p.m., U.S. President Barack Obama gave the order to attack.

The plan was to attack on Saturday, April 30, but weather was a problem. The SEALs were at an Air Base in the country of Pakistan. They had to wait. They had to be patient.

On Sunday, May 1, four helicopters flew into Abbottabad at night. Two were to land. Two were ready if needed.

Two helicopters carried 24 SEALs. Flying low, the helicopters approached the group of homes known as a **compound**. The compound was surrounded by walls 12–15 feet (4–5 m) tall and 3 feet (1 m) thick. Inside the compound was a large house. This is where the SEALs expected to find Osama bin Laden. One helicopter landed hard. No one was hurt. The SEALs attacked!

Quickly they got inside the house. Osama bin Laden's adult son was one of the first killed. The SEALs made their way to the second floor. They found a woman there. She was using her body to protect a man. The woman was shot in the leg. The man was shot in the head. He was believed to be Osama bin Laden.

The SEALs spent 30 minutes collecting computers, hard drives, and other technology. This would be used to find out more secrets about al-Qaida. The raid took less than 40 minutes. The SEALs had everything they wanted. They were ready to escape.

compound · a grouping of homes that is enclosed by a fence or wall **37**

President Obama (second from left) and his national security team nervously waited for updates during the SEAL mission.

The helicopter that made the hard landing was not able to take off. But the SEALs even had a plan for this problem. The SEALs destroyed the helicopter so it could not be used by the enemy. Then they escaped in the second helicopter.

The SEALs took the body of Osama bin Laden with them. They flew the body to a ship in the Indian Ocean. By 11 a.m. Sunday morning they had done testing on the body. The testing made sure that the SEALs had killed the leader of al-Qaida.

The Navy prepared the body for an Islamic burial. The ceremony took almost an hour. In the end, the body of Osama bin Laden was lowered into the Indian Ocean. Soon the whole world would know what the SEALs had accomplished.

The Training Never Ends!

A SEAL never stops training. There is a lot to learn. SEALS can take training in the following subjects:

Combat Medic Training	Sniper School	Language Training
Parachuting Jumpmaster Qualification	Dive Supervisor Qualification	Intelligence Analysis

A SEAL must continue to train to be prepared for any mission. New technology must be learned. New tactics must be studied. The world is always changing. A SEAL must be ready for whatever comes his way.

Tools of the Trade
On Land ...

M4A1 carbine assault rifle

assault gloves

vest with protective body armor

and At Sea

weapons go underwater too

life vest

wet suit

Read More

Besel, Jennifer M. *The U.S. Navy SEALs: The Missions.* American Special Ops. North Mankato, Minn.: Capstone Press, 2013.

Doeden, Matt. *Can You Survive in the Special Forces? An Interactive Survival Adventure.* You Choose: Survival. North Mankato, Minn.: Capstone Press, 2013.

Rose, Simon. *Navy SEALs.* U.S. Armed Forces. New York: AV2 by Weigl, 2014.

Internet Sites

FactHound offers a safe, fun way to find Internet sites related to this book. All of the sites on FactHound have been researched by our staff.

Here's all you do:
Visit *www.facthound.com*
Type in this code: 9781625210104

 Check out projects, games and lots more at **www.capstonekids.com**

Glossary
of Text Features

Text Feature	How to Use It
Caption: A word or group of words shown with a picture or illustration	Read a caption to understand information that may not be in the text.
Diagram: A drawing that shows or explains something	Examine a diagram to understand steps in a process, how something is made, or the parts of something.
Glossary: List of key terms with their meanings	Look up key terms in the glossary to find their meanings and to get a better understanding of the topic of the text.
Index: Alphabetical list of key terms, names, and topics in a text with their page numbers	Use the index to find pages that contain information you are looking for.
Map: A drawing that represents a place, such as a country or city	Use a map to understand relative locations and determine where events took place.
Photograph or Illustration: Visuals that are created by cameras or drawn	Examine photographs and illustrations to better understand ideas in the text that might be unclear.
Subhead: Word or group of words that divides the text into sections and tells the main idea of a section	Use subheads to locate information in the text and understand how a text is organized.
Table: Represents data in a small space	Examine a table to understand data or to compare information in the text.
Table of Contents: List of the major parts of the book and their page numbers	Use a table of contents to locate general information in the text and see how the topics are organized.
Text Box: A box in the text that provides extra information about a topic	Read a text box to understand interesting or important information.
Text Style: Bold, color, or italic words in the text	Pay attention to bold, italic, and color words to figure out which words in the text are important.
Timeline: Shows events in the order in which they occurred	Use a timeline to understand the order in which events occurred or how one event led to another.

Glossary

active-duty (AK-tiv DOO-tee) · working in the military now

ambush (AM-bush) · a surprise attack

amphibious (am-FI-bee-uhs) · operating on both land and water

assault (ah-SAWLT) · a sudden, violent attack

boot camp (BOOT CAMP) · a place for training new members

citizen (SI-tuh-zuhn) · a member of a country or state who has the right to live there

compound (KAHM-paund) · a grouping of separate homes that is enclosed by a fence or wall

demolition (de-muh-LI-shuhn) · blowing up or taking down a structure on purpose

elite (i-LEET) · the best of the best

embassy (EM-buh-see) · a building where representatives from another country live and work

fin (FIN) · a long, flat attachment worn on the foot to help a person swim

hijack (HYE-jak) · to take control of a vehicle by force

patrol (puh-TROL) · to walk or travel through an area to protect it or to keep watch

preparatory (PREP-uh-tor-ee) · to get ready

qualification (kwahl-uh-fuh-KAY-shuhn) • a skill or ability that makes a person prepared to do a job or task

rappel (ruh-PEL) • to slide down a strong rope

reconnaissance (ree-KAH-nuh-suhnss) • a mission to gather information about an enemy

recruit (ri-KROOT) • a new member of a group

scuba diver (SKOO-buh DIVE-ur) • a person who swims underwater with air tanks for breathing

sniper (SNY-pur) • a soldier trained to shoot at long-distance targets from a hidden place

surveillance (suhr-VAY-luhnss) • the act of keeping very close watch on someone, someplace, or something

tactic (TAK-tik) • a plan for fighting a battle

technique (tek-NEEK) • a method or way of doing something that requires skill

terrorism (TER-ur-i-zuhm) • the use of threats or force to frighten or harm others

terrorist (TER-uhr-ist) • someone who uses violence and threats to frighten people into obeying

waver (WAY-vur) • to be unsteady

weaponry (WEP-uhn-ree) • a collection of weapons

Index